TOP 10 FASTEST

Sea Animals

SHERRY HOWARD

Rourke
Educational Media
rourkeeducationalmedia.com

A Division of
Carson Dellosa Education

Before Reading: *Building Background Knowledge and Vocabulary*

Building background knowledge can help children process new information and build upon what they already know. Before reading a book, it is important to tap into what children already know about the topic. This will help them develop their vocabulary and increase their reading comprehension.

Questions and Activities to Build Background Knowledge:

1. Look at the front cover of the book and read the title. What do you think this book will be about?
2. What do you already know about this topic?
3. Take a book walk and skim the pages. Look at the table of contents, photographs, captions, and bold words. Did these text features give you any information or predictions about what you will read in this book?

Vocabulary: *Vocabulary Is Key to Reading Comprehension*

Use the following directions to prompt a conversation about each word.

- Read the vocabulary words.
- What comes to mind when you see each word?
- What do you think each word means?

Vocabulary Words:
- *bill*
- *mammal*
- *migrate*
- *rigid*
- *technology*
- *torpedo*

During Reading: *Reading for Meaning and Understanding*

To achieve deep comprehension of a book, children are encouraged to use close reading strategies. During reading, it is important to have children stop and make connections. These connections result in deeper analysis and understanding of a book.

Close Reading a Text

During reading, have children stop and talk about the following:

- Any confusing parts
- Any unknown words
- Text to text, text to self, text to world connections
- The main idea in each chapter or heading

Encourage children to use context clues to determine the meaning of any unknown words. These strategies will help children learn to analyze the text more thoroughly as they read.

When you are finished reading this book, turn to the next-to-last page for **After Reading Questions** and an **Activity**.

Table of Contents

Speedy Sea Animals

Sea animals dart through the water. Some dive.
Some soar across the surface!

Speed helps sea animals survive. Some use speed to **migrate**. Some use speed to snatch snacks. Others use speed so they won't become snacks!

Body shape, fins, and tails
all help make fish speedy.
The fastest fish have the
most forward movement with
the least drag.

10 **migrate** (MYE-grate): to move to another
area or climate at a particular time of year

7

Wahoo

This fish is one of the fastest in the sea. It has **rigid** gills. Its gills help it quickly take in oxygen as it speeds through the water.

8

10 **rigid** (RIJ-id): stiff and difficult to bend

Orca

This **mammal** is the largest of the dolphins. Its speed is surprising for its weight. It can blast out of the water to catch a seal.

Orcas are found in every ocean.

10 **mammal** (MAM-uhl): a warm-blooded animal that has fur or hair and that typically gives birth to live babies

11

Flying Fish

This fish can blast out of the water and soar across the surface. With its high, long leaps, it can land on a ship's deck!

Many fish swim in schools. A school of flying fish may include more than a million members! These groups provide protection from predators. Some fish use schools to surround and trap prey.

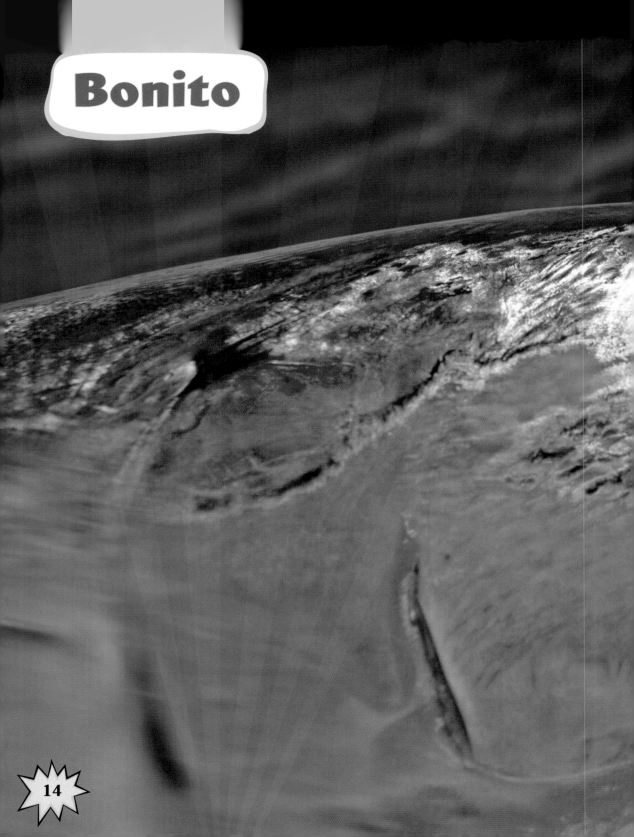

Bonito

This fish is sometimes called a *skipjack*. It can swiftly swim long distances. It is known for its high-speed leaps.

The Atlantic bonito is tinier than a pencil eraser when it is born.

Mako Shark

This shark lives in the fast lane. It can swim more than 60 miles (97 kilometers) an hour! It is the fastest shark in the world.

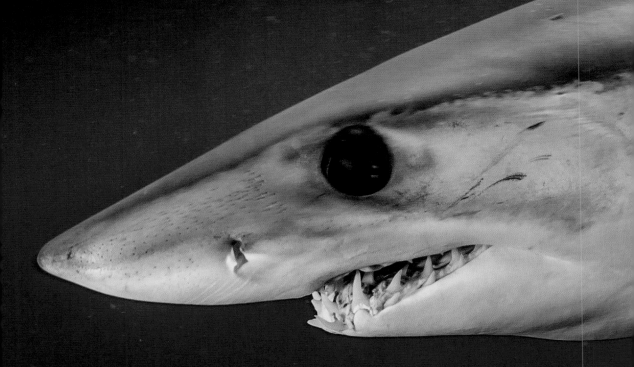

Water is denser than air. It takes a lot of power to speed through water.

Pilot Whale

This whale is called "the cheetah of the sea."
It makes top-speed, deep dives to catch food.

Pilot whales are members of the dolphin family. They are friendly and smart.

Yellowfin Tuna

This fish is big and fast. It can weigh up to 400 pounds (181 kilograms)! It uses its **torpedo** shape to rocket through the water.

10 **torpedo** (tor-PEE-doh): shaped like a tube

Blue Marlin

This fish uses its huge tail to speed away from predators. Its high-speed leap and sharp **bill** let it attack and spear prey in the air.

 bill (bil): the beak or jaws of an animal

22

Swordfish

This fish likes warm waters. It uses its speed for migration. It also uses its speed to escape hungry orcas and sharks.

Sailfish

This fish is the fastest animal in the sea! Its sail-like fins stretch almost the whole length of its body. It reaches swift speeds with its jumps.

A sailfish can reach
speeds up to 68 miles
(109 kilometers)
per hour.

27

Modern **technology** lets scientists study the deep sea. Scientists study how fast and far fish can swim. They use small devices to measure speed and distance.

10 **technology** (tek-NAH-luh-jee): the use of science and engineering to do practical things

Memory Game

Look at the pictures. What do you remember reading on the pages where each image appeared?

Index

After Reading Questions

1. Which fish is the fastest animal in the sea?

2. How do scientists study the speed of sea animals?

3. How does a blue marlin catch its prey?

4. Which fish has a torpedo shape?

5. Which animal is nicknamed "the cheetah of the sea"?

Activity

Think about how a fish's body is shaped for speed.
How could you use this as inspiration to design a car
or boat? Draw a picture of your invention.

About the Author

Sherry Howard loves the sea. She dreams of living on a beach someday. You're more likely to find her sitting in the sand than chasing fast sea animals.

www.rourkeeducationalmedia.com

PHOTO CREDITS: Cover, page1: ©CoreyFord; pages 4-5, 30: ©Elena Malysheva; pages 6-7: ©Global_Pics; pages 8-9, 30: ©Neophuket; pages 10-11, 30: ©MarkMalleson; pages 12-13, 30: ©Kemter; pages 14-15: ©seraficus; pages 16-17, 26-27, 30: ©Dmitry Kokh; pages 20-21: ©Shane Gross; pages 22-23, 30: ©Kelldallfall; pages 24-25: ©Gorb Andrii; pages 28-29: ©NOAA

Edited by: Kim Thompson
Cover and Interior design by: Kathy Walsh

Library of Congress PCN Data

Sea Animals / Sherry Howard
(Top Ten Fastest)
  ISBN 978-1-73161-463-6 (hardcover)
  ISBN 978-1-73161-264-9 (soft cover)
  ISBN 978-1-73161-568-8 (e-Book)
  ISBN 978-1-73161-673-9 (ePub)
Library of Congress Control Number: 2019932369

Rourke Educational Media
Printed in the United States of America,
North Mankato, Minnesota